DREAM TODAY, LIVE TOMORROW

JULIAN TURNER

Dream Today, Live Tomorrow

Published by: Dreamshine Books
www.dreamshinemedia.com

Printed in the United States of America
First Printing

ISBN-13: 978-0692230039

CONTENTS

ALIVE

I arise, calm as the sun sets over the
sea on a summer day.
Eyes vibrant with color like
the sky after rain.
I'm alive...fresh air flows in
and cool breath blows out.
Mind energized, powered
by positive thinking.

The world is a wondrous creation,
A gift from God.
His light illuminates the vast
landscape of life, like the shadow from
the highest mountain blankets
 over the masses below.

Through His spirit wisdom flows like a mighty wind.
I seek solace in solitude surrounded by his presence.
As the river runs deep in the delta, so does my faith in God rest in the depths of my soul.
I arise, blessed beyond measure.
Thankful for sight to see, ears to hear, and a heart to love unconditionally.
I'm alive.

MARATHON DREAMS

The weeks just go by
They come and they go,
they come and they go,
they come and they...
The transition is swift between this
day and that day,
this season and that season
I need time to slow down
My life is running 360, which I'm
moving at a quarter of
I can't front, cruising fast
but still feel so behind
Playing catch up with destiny

Tired of living in my dreams

It's time for my dreams to live in me
Now I don't trust myself, I trust God
No more steps of hesitation
Only leaps of faith
I've seen my future past the present
Life is a marathon, and greatness
waits at the finish line
Only two options:
Complete it, or be defeated

BELIEVE YOU CAN, KNOW YOU WILL

Believe you can, Know you will
Effort is Everything
Passion is Persistence
Don't Means Do
Stop Means Go
Fight Fear with Faith
Let Doubt Die
Live life limitless

THUNDER IN MY HEAD

*T*hunder roars inside a closed box
Moving like a rapid train, thoughts
are trapped inside my brain
No escape from this eternal
internal discourse
Minutes feel like hours,
and hours feel like days
I descend into a daze

My only freedom is focus,
but I'm stuck on repeat
My healing is hopeless,
feeling trapped in defeat

I need a vision breakthrough to
expand my mindsight
In hindsight, I need reinvention
to get my mind right

Pleasures of life are skewed by anxiety
Purpose uncharged is
fueled in sobriety
I want to live in the moment
of excellence, not die in
a sea of mediocrity
I'm pushing ahead past my problems
to a life with greener pastures
I was locked in my head until I
knocked the door down
Took the lid of the box, and my
thunder wore down

CONNECTION

Complexity.
Diverse intricate pieces
of life connected
I stand tall above the
giants of adversity
Head held high, fear fallen low

I ponder the moment when dreams
upgrade from abstract concepts
to concrete creations.
The set up of greatness is aligned
with pure power of persistence
I fight my inner enemy as it attempts
to disconnect my mighty fortitude
Failure is a false identity,
but success is truth

I'm breathing in the realness of faith
Surrendering to God's plan
Alone I lose, but when
linked with divine favor,
victory is the only outcome

From myself I'll only accept
excellence, no exception
I'm flowing forward, one direction
Going toward, new affection
Love and Life, twin goals
Connection
Heartbeats at the beach
where the wind blows
Perfection

DREAM TODAY, LIVE TOMORROW

I rode the waves across
the sea of despair
I once cried tears of hopeless sorrow
I dream today, I live tomorrow

I feel the calming light of summer
I braved the thunderous winter
I once cried tears of hopeless sorrow
I dream today, I live tomorrow

My mind is transformed, made anew
My heart was lost
My joy is found
I once cried tears of hopeless sorrow
I dream today, I live tomorrow

THE JOURNEY

It's the little things that have the
biggest impact on our lives
The wind blows past faces
uninterrupted by human interest
Yet the wind carries the breathe of life
We feed off the belly of nature
Yet turn a blind eye to
the needs of the world

The farmer plants the seed
and waits for the earth
to nourish it into fruit
Fruit can't grow in tainted soil
Life gives birth to miracles
but greatness doesn't
develop in mediocrity

Action is effort that leads
toward the path of success
Inaction is a wasted opportunity
which leaves you drowning
in a well of failure

Growth is defined by gradual change
Stagnation is progressive suicide
Life is an epic road of self-discovery
and joy is hidden in the journey
We must move forward for happiness
or crawl backwards towards despair
Our destinies are determined
by the decisions we make

ENDINGS

Don't focus on what was,
focus on what will be
Change is divorcing the past,
and marrying the future
New Life is growth through death
We must accept that
progress is a process
In order to proceed
we must push through struggle
Each day carries something more
than the day before
We must embrace endings
For they are the
catalysts for transitions

THE TEST

In deep waters I swim blindly
Up rocky mountains I
climb unharnessed
My fear is sacrificed for peace
I find comfort through enduring
the uncomfortable

Moments come I doubt my calling
Faith moves me forward
Battles fought with wins and losses
I see victory in my war with destiny

When all is done I feel complete
I passed my test
I conquered defeat

MOMENTS THAT
I LIVE

I laugh, I cry, I love, I give
My journey is defined,
in moments that I live
I accept the struggles my
heart must bear
I carry weight and push through fear
I pray, I listen, I plan, I do
I walk this path in faith,
where will it lead me to?

LETTER TO MY FORMER SELF

Dear old me,
Just thinking about you
Days ago I lived in darkness
Cold nights I cried alone
No life, I died alone

Sad to see my hopeless state
Trapped in my mind, hopeless fate
Hated myself, no love there
Pain inside, overflowed with fear

Hey Old Me, I don't miss you
I've moved away from your issue
I'm a New Me, free from the past
I've been fortified, rebuilt to last

TOMORROW,
FOREVER

T ouched...there's a feeling I'm feeling
My heart's revealing
this emotional healing
Is it L.O.V.E?
Possibly, but definitely positive
I live with brighter smiles
My mind's rejuvenated
My body is lighter now
Wow...could it be that I'm
no longer thirsty?

I've tasted happiness,
drank from her well
I'm nourished by the raw essence of
her eternal beauty

Her being is beyond perfection
I feel a special bond, connection
Her soul ignites my ambition
Her heart invites my passion
Yesterday ended early
Tomorrow will be better
I pray together we will grow
Tomorrow, forever

WHERE GOD RESTS

Follow your heart, feed your soul
Grace and love, so beautiful
Mercy falls on the merciful
Heaven waits beyond this earth
When darkness falls, light is birthed

Life begins after death
Self-surrender brings lasting breath
Peace is made by the Potter
He guides the path
through open water

Live for purpose, not for power
Live for service, not for honor
Blessed are those who live to bless
Joy is found where God rests

I (EYE)

I think, I see, I plan, I try
If I fail, my efforts multiply
I walk, I run, I jump, I fly
Today I awake my fearless eye
My faith, my dreams,
my mind, my fight
They all in whole, define my life

SORRY,
I'M NOT PERFECT

Sorry, I'm not perfect
The price of life is sacrifice
Can't decide if this is worth it

Eyes in the sky, feet on the ground
Lost hope dreaming
Uncertainty I found
Prayed for peace and clarity
Confidence came around

Vision with purpose
Greatness I see
Sorry, I'm not perfect
But today I'm a better me

DEAR CATERPILLAR

Dear Caterpillar,
Please don't cry
You ask why?
Someday you'll die and
become a butterfly
The heart grows through pains
Life lived fully equals losses plus gains
Success feels like standing still
in the face of fear
The lights come on and
a bell rings near
The end is where YOU begin

RECOVERY

Sometimes seasons of life
all seem the same
Winter nights never change
Spring is lost in darkness
Hope drowns in the rain

Light hides like a speck of dust
in a crowded room
Trees branch into the soil,
but they never bloom
In times of toil, hearts grow hard
and minds cloud with gloom

So how can we see recovery?
Swim high in the sea of lows
Cut down the barren fig in the field
Plant a healthy tree that grows

THE SICKNESS

Life is living to give
Sacrifice is dying to live
Open hands feed the flock
With open minds their needs unlock
Although some see hope clearly, this
view is not the norm
Some reach out with help,
but others won't perform
Love without cost is FREEdom

Hate is the price of rejection
There's a sickness in society...
An obsession with possession
The cure is developed
with a pure heart
It's time we start to analyze our lives

Do I have more than I need?
Or do I need more than I have?
Is my satisfaction a
sustained reality?
Or is it just an eternal dream
fueled from greed?

REFLECTION IN
THE SUN

One summer day in the heat of June,
I step outside, on the border of
evening and afternoon
My bare feet rub against
the warm concrete
I walk with both arms out
in front of me
The bright sunlight is stunning me
Beautiful shades of the rays,
I'm amazed abundantly

Here I stand in awe,
feeling blessed beyond measure
Found treasure in my soul
when I was lost in the desert

Now I'm rich in spirit,
overflowing with love
Even if I live a lowly life, my strength
comes from above

I REST MY EYES ON THE MOUNTAINTOP

I rest my eyes on the mountaintop
When dawn's upon the land,
I stand elevated
I rest my eyes on the mountaintop
A forecast of freedom lies ahead
My mind's led to a place
where I find peace
I rest my eyes on the mountaintop
Secluded from worry and pain
Water falls from above,
my body is cleansed in rain
I rest my eyes on the mountain top

THOUGHTS

Prosperity is in Peace
Life is Love
Ego is emptiness
Fear is False Faith
The one who journeys blindly
walks in the darkness of failure
The one who journeys with clear sight
walks in the light of success
Don't fear obstacles, embrace them
Obstacles are nothing more
than life's tests designed to
strengthen ones fortitude

NOTHING IS WASTED

Morning, I wake peacefully
in the shadow of dawn
Scented air seeps through
a cracked window
Intoxicating fragrance from
 flowers in the garden
A moment of meditation to
focus my mind
Silence in the room like
a barren forest

As the sun begins to rise
light ignites inside this
sanctuary of solitude
It's time to journey from
my world to a foreign land

Chasing dreams that run
faster than me
Speed is what I need
but I feed on mediocrity
Starvation from standard living
sets the course for
the marathon ahead
Stamina evolves from
effort and effective action

One step forward on
the path of progress
Eyes set north running
blind through a pit of vipers
Pushing past the poisonous bites
No time to dwell on death,
I'm fueled by life
This is just the beginning
of the battle

Committed to this race
'til the maze ends
Transformation turn by turn
Each move made brings new
meaning to the journey
Sprinting closer and closer to the
finish line, then I finally arrive
I breathe a million breaths
One for each step required
of me to get here
I'm overcome with a feeling of freedom
Released from my dreams
and destiny fulfilled
Gave all of myself to the world
I started full, I ended empty
Nothing is wasted when
 everything is sacrificed

THE SHORT ROAD
TO DISTANT DREAMS

Fresh air and new opportunities
live outside a cemetery of dead dreams
Release from captive consciousness
creates the catalyst for change
Mirrors in the mind reflect a
new perspective of potential
See yourself through yourself
Be yourself in the purest form

Find the truth of purpose
Journey through the narrow road
into the fire of hope
Belief builds the
foundation for freedom
Faith is an iron sword
forged from the heart

Guard your spirit closely as you
battle against defeat
The short road is the wrong way
The long road is the right way
Distance determines dedication
How far will you go to be great?

How many steps will you take to
reach the mountaintop?
How deep will you dig
to find your treasure?
Will your struggle be
worth the reward?
Dreams are devoid of value
and die without sacrifice
Give everything to your pursuits, and
you will be transformed in the process

FLYING WITHOUT WINGS

Two dirty feet on a raggedy sheet
A young boy paints
on cracked concrete
Born in the street with
no place to call home

Feeling lost in the world
where he was left to die
His mother was a slave
to getting high
Trapped on the expressway
to her grave
She wanted to turn her life around,
but couldn't be saved

The orphan child starts
life in the wild
Searching for meaning in the dark
His thoughts create light
that sparks inspiration
His dreams are the air
which gives breath to imagination

Born on the bottom,
now he's reaching for the sky
Born without wings,
yet he's still learning to fly
He was predicted to fall
and encouraged to never try

Five years later the odds were beat
Two clean feet on a white satin sheet
The orphan prodigy paints a
masterpiece on a slab of concrete

SPIRIT OF WONDER

Spirit of wonder, take me under
Cover me with love
Give me shelter in your shadow
Protect me from above

Illuminate my mind when
loneliness darkens the day
Paint your vibrant rainbows on
the canvas of the sky
Guide me through the valley
to the mountain peak
Show me where the river flows
toward the path of peace

Spirit of wonder, take me under
Cover me with love
Give me shelter in your shadow
Protect me from above

Here I stand in you're presence enamored
Gratitude I offer up for pulling me
from troubled waters
Days In the desert I nearly
drowned in depression
Moments standing on the cliff edge you
pushed me back to life

Spirit of wonder, take me under
Cover me with love
Give me shelter in your shadow
Protect me from above

Now I rest inside your heart
It's beautiful beat brings me joy
I smile, I dance and sing your praise
You fixed my broken wings
I'm soaring to new levels
Higher than I could ever dream

A NIGHT
WITH DESTINY

It's nightfall in the delta of desire
A girl sits still in an oak tree
 gazing at the galaxy
The wind shakes leaves
onto the grass below
A breeze blows through
the girl's brown hair
Glowing stars radiate
across the amber sky
The universe is vibrant
with opportunity

Her name is Destiny and she's
focused on a destination
She's past being in the present because
her dreams are trapped in the future

A voice inside her mind brought her
here to this place of reflection
A vision was revealed that showed
her a better life
One where she was sailing the seas
of greatness as a captain

A call was received, and she
answered without hesitation
The choice was simple,
do more, or be the same
Now tonight in the delta
she prepares for transformation
She gathers inspiration
from the clouds
Her thoughts plan
the path to progression
Night ends and day begins by
bringing in the sunlight

Destiny climbs down from the oak
tree and gets into her boat
She travels down the river toward her
destination

CITY OF SALVATION

Stranded outside a wall
in a strange land
Surrounded by a sea of quick sand
Don't know how not to sink
If I want to survive,
then maybe I should think
No light means no way out in sight
If I stay in the dark
then I'll face doom
If I don't escape soon I'll go insane
Worse would be a curse on my soul
Can't quit now need to
step into stronger role
Hard to admit I'm scared to fail
The strength I show is just a veil

When weakness makes me weary
salty eyes turn teary
Yet despite my fear I refuse to fall
I decide to stand tall against
the wall of adversity
I push past my problem and immerse
in a city salvation

LA DI DADA

A cool Friday afternoon
It's the middle of June
I hear the birds singing
La Di Dada La Di Dada
Happiness is in the air
Vision I see clear
Altitude is so high
Sitting on a rainbow blowing
bubbles in the sky
I hear angels singing
La Di Dada La Di Dada
The sound is soft and sweet
An intoxicating melodic treat
Like vanilla kisses in my ear
Oh what a wonderful time of the year
I hear the trumpets blowing
La Di Dada La Di Dada

My heart is dancing to the beat
My mind is peaceful on retreat
I want to share this feeling
Healing through the mood of music
Break the mold of despair, let your
spirit rise above the ceiling

ELEVATED IMAGERY

These words were birthed
on a mountain peak
Elevated imagery
translated metaphorically
Capturing the essence of
the atmosphere up here
Breath of cool air on my neck as I pray
The scent of the earth surrounds me
Smiling at the vista of the horizon
Vibrant colors in the clouds
paint a picture of perfection
Nature is a living museum of beauty
I stand in awe with eyes wide open
Mesmerized by the intricate details of this
mountain masterpiece

CALL TO COMPLETION

Quiet in a place with my face
in my hands listening to the song
of the wind calling me calmly
get up and go forward
no turning back
step into your dreams
with both feet planted like a tree in the
earth stay the course
opposition in my way
I wanna stop but need to lead my present
self to my future self
no time for rest time to study for the test
ahead on the hill
I will persevere in this battle
I know the path on which I walk

I've seen it in my visions perfect picture
in my mind
success is such a freeing feeling
far from where I've been
I made it here with some scars
but strengthened from the war
now I am complete

TENETS 1
THROUGH 7

*Limitlessness is power that breaks
through false barriers of the mind.
The embryo of inspiration is
incubated in visionary thinking.
Fear and doubt are the anchors of
restrained passions.
Faith and boldness break the chains
of creative confinement.
Wisdom is crucial to conquering the
traps of delusion.
Truth is found in seeking with
an open mind.
Belief without thought or action
is self-deception.*

SLOW DOWN

Where are you?
I'm in this conversation by myself
wondering where my mind went
racing thoughts cloud my head
claustrophobia from the chaos
confused by this environment
feel like I'm drowning in
a polluted pond
thirsting for fresh water
please give me a sip
before I slip into a coma
I'm losing my sense of self
seeing familiar things I
don't recognize
everything is moving too fast
need time to
slow....down

ILLUSION

This must be Deja Vu
Seems like the same situation I went
through a year ago
September came and went
Then again I spent energy
on bad habits
None of which I will mention
A few were mundane but most
were crazy enough to drive me insane
Living in the shadows of sin
seeking thrills
Highs and lows
Found regret in the valleys
Shame in the hills
Lost in a world I created for myself
Alone on an island of illusion

Waiting to wake up from this
nightmare of confusion
One night in my room I
heard a voice in my head
It said open your eyes to see the light
Reject your wrongs
and accept my path as right
I awoke on a cliff with elevated height
Vision became clear
I had brand new sight

FREE

With bent knees
I pray for strength
Sometime pain feels like
 too much to bear
Never ending struggles strangle me
Fresh air is freedom
Love is freedom
Peace is freedom
Freedom
That's what I'm seeking
Trapped in my mind
I need to escape this prison
Life is beautiful on the outside
Inside everything seems cloudy
This battle drains my spirit

I look to God for release
He can see the bigger
picture of my reality
My vision is skewed
with discontentment
Something is missing
I want more
More joy
More life
More purpose
More freedom from emotions
that consume me
I'll keep praying and fighting
until I am released
My future will be free

THE WAITING WIDOW

A widow sits on a chair
by the side of the road
silently observing the caravan of cars
cruising up the mountain
A young smiling face pokes out the
window of a white wagon
He's a boy on a solo journey exploring
the world with wide eyes
He waves at the widow
She smiles and returns the gesture
She knows where he's going
She travelled up this route before
Many times
This endless road has made her old
She's pursued her dream at the
highest altitude on earth

During every trip she lost her grip
on the Mountain Of Perseverance
She slipped down and
turned back around
to the place where she began
Now she sits in her chair thinking
about when she'll start
her journey again
All day she watches travelers
as they embark up the road
She hopes someone will stop
and ask her for directions
Maybe one day she can help
someone be the first to
complete their journey
Until then the widow waits for the
strength to finish what
she started long ago

SOMETIMES I CRY

What happened to all the roses?
Sometimes I cry in
my garden at night
Tears flow for dead flower buds
Why did the sunshine die?
Crickets cry outside my window
They hold funerals under dark skies
My reality seems so surreal
If truth is in emotions then
depression never lies
Staring at the black walls
while lying in bed
Head filled with thoughts
that weigh me down
Having a hard time letting
up this emotion

Then I hear a wind chime
in my window
Mesmerizing music brings
me peace and release
Blind to pain cut off from captivity
and covered with clarity
A clear mind gives sight of
a future fulfilled
Living in HD on hill
with panoramic views
Red roses blooming in every season
Nights and days no matter the time
sunshine always stays
I still cry sometimes but now there's
joy in those tears

DIRECTIONS IN A WHISPER

Sleep at the base off a waterfall
Awakened by a whisper in my ear
A call is what I hear
Hurry and go
Heed these directions
Don't move slow
Pace will set the tone
for the journey ahead
Don't look back
Focus forward instead
Be careful and seek guidance
through the raging river
No help is no hope is negligent

Wanderers in cold water
shiver to death
Pray the prayer of life to
be delivered from death
Never travel alone facing
obstacles of fear
Never navigate heavy storms
using blind eyes to steer
Wisdom is power
Ignorance is failure
Go forth and find your way

FAMILIAR SMOKE

I step into an elevator
greeted by a familiar smell
toxic kush that burned my eyes
gave my lungs hell
a nightmare disguised as a fantasy
reality was I was killing myself
with smoke on my mind I lost
sense of hope feeling like I fell
from a ledge on the edge of death
with each breath I inhaled demons
tormenting my soul crying out
to God please free me from
the prison of this pipe
I'm suffering in suffocation losing
sight of the future

Lord please bring me back
I'm done
tired of fighting by myself
alone this battle can't be won

TROUBLED WATER

It all ends when it started
5 o'clock on the dock in the rain
with a watch on his wrist counting
down to the crash of his downfall
he was moving up in the world 'til his
soul slipped on the ladder of morality
then he lost it all
now everything is chaos
constant struggle in the bubble
of his mind menacing emotions
have him floating on a gray cloud
feeling empty in this daze looking at
the water wondering how to
erase painful memories
shame stained upon his heart
hurting inside

waiting for a savior to set him free
from his pool of pity
he edges closer to the dock's edge
A step and 3 seconds from
stopping his sorrow
he picks up the phone
ringing in his pocket
answering the call from
a girl distressed
by the long letter that he wrote her
"wish I could give you more"
is what he told her
she said she loved him
unconditionally and didn't
care about his demons
cause he was her daddy
so she needed his affection
and protection
she begged him "please don't do it!"

after she cried out
he changed his mind
too much to take he couldn't go to
sleep in the bay
leaving his family awake in misery
he stepped away from the water
and went home to his daughter

OUTSIDE

1 hear the smooth piano playing
meditating to the music
in a moment of bliss.
Smiling as 1 look out the window.
Midnight seemed desolate
but this morning is a miracle.
Captivating creatures showcase
the beauty of nature.
Butterflies and lilies pose
in symbiotic harmony.
I'm inspired by this
authentic connection.
Gaining new perspective on
old opposing thoughts.

Meaningful relationships felt foreign.
Love felt like a leopard running.
Heart hunted quick and deadly,
body turned heavy
and feverishly consumed.
Yet in death I gained life
through a new lens.
Now I'm seeing truth on the outside.
Outside my window where the
butterflies and lilies live.
Together

COST OF COMPLETION

I'm in this race until it ends
Life begins when a choice
is made to breathe
Seeds planted in soil breed dreams
I fight against time to bear fruits
Harvesting in fragile gardens
trying not to tear roots
Decisions I make are elevating
With every new position I take
I'm celebrating
Thankful for progress in this process
Advancing mile by mile
no longer novice

Hurdles make me stronger
The longer I move forward
the closer I come toward
the finish line
This isn't over, but I'm almost there
Completion requires a cost, a price
that isn't always clear

UNTIL VICTORY IS WON

Why is life so complicated?
Raging rivers I cross with broken oars
Feeling lost and overwhelmed
Heavy heart weighs me down
Searching for the right answer
to the wrong question
When will I get better?
No, how will I get better?
Pain is a process
In each level there's perseverance
I'm elevated closer to the end
Then I can begin
the process of healing
Then I can grow into the mold
I was designed for
Every day I'm looking forward

Leaving dark energy behind me
Forgetting bad memories
that try to remind me
of nights when I cried alone
Empty in a home without lights
Today I might fall,
but tomorrow I will
stand up again and fight
The battle continues
until victory is won

EDGE OF DESPAIR

Dropped so many tears
I just can't cry no more
Wondering where my mind went
Too much time spent in my head
Almost dead to life but still breathing
Toxic emotions keep seething
Feeling stuck in a state of waste
I try to move with haste
toward a better place
Need to face my demons
 time to awake
Sick of worthless pursuits
Sick of stress that drives me crazy
I can't think I need a drink
No I don't I need a sink
To cleanse my thoughts
Polluted with anxiety

Pressure pushes me to the edge
I'm fighting on a ledge
Daily decisions to be made
I pray for wisdom in this wilderness
Walking without direction
Afraid to wander into despair
I'll keep walking till I
reach a destination
Where I'm destined I desire to be
My vision is weak so my sight is dark
If I make it through the fire
I will see clearly

SWIMMING ASLEEP

My spirit is definitely in a deficit
Lately I've been down
deep in the dark
asleep in a somber state
My soul waits for rehabilitation
dreaming of a life without worry
Thinking why should I die
in a womb of anxiety
Depression I embrace face forward
swimming in a salty sea of tears
searching for sanity
Losing feeling in my feet
I'm afraid of drowning
Losing vision in my eyes
I'm afraid of blindness
Looking for a lighthouse
Need guidance out this dark water

There's a figure in the distance
I can't seem to see it's face
A voice guides me to the shore
Moments later I awake

TENETS 8 THROUGH 12

Polluted water propagates a rich apple seed into poor fruit.

Desire lays dormant in the depths of a diluted mind.

The path of purpose purifies the conscious puzzle.

A focused future is formed with faith and fluid action.

Motivation is a mental shift in which thoughts move beyond the margin's of self-defeat.

PEACE IN THE
PRISON OF PAIN

Blurry visions in the
mirrors of the mind
I rewind thoughts to play them back
Memories of moments I was free
Now I'm held captive to emotions
that persecute me
This inner battle is draining my soul
An enemy hides inside my head
Fighting against shadows of myself
Trying to live in the light
I dread days when the sun dies
With no sunrise I only see grey clouds
The air is too cold I can't stay out
No heat, no shelter,
nowhere to lay out
I try to retreat to my comfort zone

It's too late

Enclosed in a cave of conflict

Caged like a convict

Release is only found through peace

I'm still searching for calm weather

Until I find healing I'll

weather the storm

It's hard work working wounded

But strength is acquired

through pain

Strain makes me strong

Faith makes me sane

Every challenge has a cost

Though some things are lost

In every loss there's gain

APRIL 9TH

A special day
I am blessed to be born
Life is a gift I accept with open arms
Saw some situations
that brought me low
But even in despair my head was
raised up to the sky
Learned the sun still shines
in the dark
Looking through the clouds
 toward the light
Almost hopeless but my focus
was shifted to faith
Transformed to a vibrant man
Full of love appreciating
the little moments
Quiet time brings me comfort

Found peace in poetry
Music motivates my mind
Free to dream big
Sometimes visions are overwhelming
Truth makes me speechless
Future is reality
Greatness is evident
Everyday I'm moving forward
Growth is eternal
Internal and external
Living limitless
I'm awake

ABOUT THE AUTHOR

An award-winning published poet since high school, Julian Turner has always had a gift and passion for creative writing. Julian seeks to inspire readers to live their best lives and pursue their dreams with unyielding perseverance, no matter the circumstances.

After experiencing a life change post college, Julian became withdrawn and suffered from depression. During his dark period of emotional anguish, Julian found healing through poetry and developed a mission to help and inspire others through their emotional struggles. Julian currently resides in Los Angeles, CA.

www.ingramcontent.com/pod-product-compliance
Lightning Source LLC
Chambersburg PA
CBHW051701090426
42736CB00013B/2475